The Modified Village

The Intentional Repositioning for Children to Succeed on Purpose

Written by Rufus H. Reddick, III.

Edited by Christina L. Bullock

Bless you brother!
Enjoy the read...

Editorial Note:

Even at the cost of violating grammatical rules, we have chosen to capitalize Youth Ministry and related names. We have also chosen to keep a conversational tone to the piece to maintain the voice of the author. Italicized phrases of text throughout the work are thoughts and commentary provided as an aside to the reader from the author. Unless otherwise indicated, all Scripture quotations are from the Holy Bible, New American Standard Version. All Scripture quotations marked (KJV) are from the Holy Bible, King James Version.

Editor Information:
Christina L. Bullock
Sterling, Virginia
cbullock.wm@gmail.com

The Modified Village: The Intentional Repositioning for Children to Succeed on Purpose

Woodbridge, VA 22191
Rufus.Reddick3@gmail.com

ISBN: 13:978-1-943409-02-0

Table of Contents

DEDICATION

First I give honor to God who is at the center of my life!
I would like to dedicate this book to my Father in heaven who gave me life, breath and vision to write this book.
To my father, Pastor John Snell and my mother Dorothy R. Snell who raised me wonderfully, thank you for showing me what faith in action looks like.
To my wife Tiara Reddick, my son Rufus Reddick IV., and my baby girl Reagan Reddick whom I love very much——thank you for your inspiration and encouragement throughout this journey.
To my father in ministry, Reverend, Dr. Jerome A. Barber who saw something in me I never saw in myself.
To my Sixth Mount Zion Youth Ministry family and to the Loudoun Bible Church student ministry family...thank you. You have equipped me with the tools needed to gather the information God breathed through me on these pages.
Brace yourself because God is going to do something amazing for you if you just open your heart and allow Him to speak through the words God specifically gave me just for you.

FOREWORD

I have had the opportunity to work, pray, mentor, and learn from this outstanding young man. I have clearly been blessed by his insight, internal motivation, his relationship with God, and his love of helping and praying with people, particularly touching the lives of young people. In this book, he shares information and effective practices to help anyone who parents a child, teaches children, coaches a team, and serves as a mentor. Rev. Reddick clearly highlights in this powerful book, we are investing in our greatest resource, our youth. This is reading that should be read if you are committed to making a difference in the lives of others. In addition, the information delivered in the book is both researched based and gathered from experience. Theory is good, but experience is great. Mr. Rufus Reddick is man of God, a unique spiritual leader, and understands the concept; service to others is the rent we pay for our existence here on earth.

Carlton Ashby, M.Ed.
Educator
VSBA School Board Member
Education Consultant

SPECIAL ENDORSEMENTS

"The Modified Village"

MY WIFE

The Modified Village is a book berthed from God who has utilized a vessel to remind us that our Villages are not dead--they just need to be revived. Buckle your seatbelts for this journey to be challenged, repositioned and empowered as a parent to re-establish a legacy for your children to have for generations to come!

Tiara A. Reddick

MY FATHER

With all that I've learned at home, I thank God for my surroundings. Those who scolded me when my mother was not around and for the old lady who went out of her way to find out who my mother was, to tell her she didn't like the crowd I was hanging around. Without that guidance I would not be the man that I am today. WHAT A BLESSING! I am living proof that the village is still the answer.

Pastor John Snell

St. John Baptist Church

Cleveland, Ohio

MY MOTHER

Colossians 3:20. The Bible says Children are to obey their parents IN ALL THINGS (which includes honesty, love, trust, loyalty, devotion and forgiveness) for this is well pleasing unto the Lord. In this book you will be amazed at the way my baby-boy explains the village concept but through a modified approach for the 21st century parent. Be blessed by this book.

Dorothy R. Snell

MY PASTOR

(Father in Ministry)

A fresh look at an age old challenge of raising the best children in a tough society. The Modified Village lifts up every stone to expose the underlying strategies to corrupt the next generation, but leaves the reader with a renewed sense of hope and strength in God's power working through us to save our children.

Pastor, Dr. Jerome A. Barber

Sixth Mount Zion Baptist Temple

Hampton, Virginia

ENDORSEMENTS

This book can revitalize our villages and help us raise up the next generation together. The Modified Village is a must have.

- Pastor Judah and Tiffany Early

Parents of two children

To the family of believers--I want to personally encourage you to support this great young author Rufus Reddick in his endeavors to strengthen and encourage us as a community and family to work together in love to assist our children in navigating the early part of their lives. In remembering what it took for us, we know what it'll take for them. It will take a village. Let's buy, read, gift, and apply these teachings.

- Pastor C. A. Burns Sr.

Father

Pastor Reddick gets it! He unfolds the village concept while yet placing emphasis on God and family! He also invites us into an environment of "the farmer" by explaining the concept of planting seeds! This body of information is a must read…

- Rev. Hosea and Janet Fitten

Parents of three children

With so many challenges and changes within our families, parenting has become more difficult than ever. The end result is that our kids need greater care and nurturing to become successful and productive people. These persons offer a relevant, practical and meaningful model of raising children in this generation. A model that should not be ignored, but embraced by our churches and most of all--communities.

- Pastor, Dr. Kevin G. Swann

Father of two children

The Modified Village is a book that resonates with parenting instincts that offers concrete and achievable guidelines for parenting. It is apparent that there is no quick fix to successful parenting, but Rufus Reddick's holistic approach provides a framework which helps to enhance the development of our children.

This book is a reminder that those of us who have achieved some measure of success is because we were surrounded with caring, nurturing, and loving adults. The Modified Village is a must read for those who truly believe that everybody is God's somebody.

- Pastor Eddie W. Lawrence

Father of two children

Rufus possesses a unique insight of today's family and the issues they face. His approach is spiritually based and carefully thought out. This book provides the current generation of parents some much needed answers to the problems that some face. He understands that today's fast-moving society poses unique issues for parents that require an entire village to resolve. I believe that The Modified Village should be a must read for parents and those individuals willing to invest in our future. I salute his efforts!

- Alexander and Shirley Norwood

Parents of two children and Grandparents of three children

It truly takes a village to raise a child. They are God's Angels here in earth.

- Glenn and Felita Fields

Parents of three children and grandparents of eight children

Modified Village is a beautiful and distinct montage that exudes the aroma of Christ. This book helps us realize a powerful truth: we all have been guilty of praying for rain, but have not prepared our fields. Rufus Reddick III's brilliance is consistent as he spiritually awakens the rhythm of humanity, by speaking light into every broken heart and beautiful mind. Modified Village brings value to how our children view tomorrow and how tomorrow will view them.

- Carl and Shaterria Dixon

Parents of three children

This book is a must read. The bible tells us in Proverbs 22:6 to; "Train up a child in the way he should go; even when he is old he will not depart from it." But in today's modern age the reality is that is not always the case. We can be the best parents; in our eyes do everything right and our children still stray. As a single parent of three beautiful children I've learned over the course of time and error that I could not have raised them all on my own. It was only by the grace of God and a number of select individuals that God placed in my life that I have deemed as my village, that I am able to say that this journey of parenting has thus far been successful. Rufus Reddick III has been an integral part of my village for several years providing spiritual guidance and support to both myself and my children. It is through my personal experience that I can attest that, the village is the answer. Rufus along with others have acted as angels watching over me when I alone did not have all the answers. I highly recommend this book to be used as a source of comfort and strength to parents who may feel as if they are in this alone my prayer is that as you read this book that you are given fresh revelation that it does take a village to raise a child. It's team work that makes the dream work!

- Amega Bland

Single mother of three children

Children who have the love of a parent plus the love of a village equal the cultivation of confidence and self-assurance that radiates spiritually from within.

- Karen Fauntleroy

Single mother of one child

Speaking straight from the heart, Rufus Reddick takes us back home with his ideals on raising our children with a Biblical perspective. He reels you in with hilarious references from his own upbringing under the traditions of "it takes a village" and gets right to the core of the problems without hesitation. His brutal honesty cuts through all of the fog and clearly paints a path for us parents to change our methods in order to produce a stronger and wiser God-fearing generation of children. I'm grateful for his clarity and wisdom.

- Lindsay Fenner

Single mother of one child

Rufus Reddick's captivating use of language inspires both parents and future parents alike. He reminds us that we're not alone in the trials that come with raising children. He reminds us that it still takes a village

- Vena Reed

College student at VCU

Chapter One

Who Can You Trust?

Trust nothing but God and keep your eyes on everything.

An old African Proverb is often attributed to this famous phrase: “It takes a village to raise a child.” No one truly knows where the phrase originates, but most leaders and youth groups have tapped into this mindset. I remember my mother telling me about the times when being a child was fun and safe at the same time. She would sit my sister and I down and share with us how different neighborhoods were when she was growing up. She was able to go anywhere in the neighborhood and her parents would not worry about her whereabouts. The trust parents had in the community was amazing to me as I sat with my sister, tuned in to every word my mother was saying. She would go on to mention how it never mattered how far she strayed away from home,

> Big mama’s hand was just like the blood of Jesus; it could reach to the highest mountain and flow to the

lowest valley. "Everything you do outside of this house will still be reported back to me so you better not embarrass me or our family name," Big mama would say.

See, in those days no wrong could be done without someone in your vicinity saying they knew your grandfather or your grandmother. I can only imagine if it was like this today. Everywhere I'd go all I would hear is, "Are you Dorothy's son?" Or in my mom's case, "Are you one of them Robinsons?" There was not a place in town that did not recognize one of the kids in the neighborhood in those wonderfully community-driven days. There was not a crime you could commit that your parents would not hear about before you got home. There was no limit to how many lashes you may have gotten if someone caught you acting up outside of your parent's home. If my mother got into trouble and an adult from the community was present, she would receive a "good behind whooping" right then and there. Afterward, that parent in the community would call her mom and she would get another spanking when she got home.

Boy I tell you, the good 'ole days!

Those were definitely times when kids could be kids but also a time where parents were able to be parents. We live in a totally different world today. These days, if you say something to a child that is not your own you just might get a good cursing out—not only by the child in question, but also by the parent. Even if the child was totally disrespectful to you, it still probably would not matter because some parents believe their child can do no wrong. In these cases it is challenging to blame the child alone without somewhat understanding it must also be the ignorance of the parent.

This is why I personally do not believe in a "bad child." On the contrary I have seen parents allow their challenges to negatively influence their child to become just as crazy as they are. Now, there are some who might disagree with this statement due to those children who were exposed to nothing but great things and still decided to go down a path of pure disappointment. Even though this may be true, I still believe that behavior is learned whether it is good or bad. So, whatever the outcome of a child, the child learned that behavior from somewhere under the leadership of his or her parent. This behavior could have been taught through the parent allowing certain family members or friends who do not have the same mindset as the parent to watch the child because there was no one else at the time. This behavior could have been taught through the parent not monitoring the type of teaching that television instilled in the child. Parents must realize that whatever your child watches on television has to be monitored the majority of the time.

A lot of parents that I have encountered who call themselves "managing television sitcoms in their home," are still in most cases dropping the ball. Think about it. What these parents find themselves doing is only watching a few episodes of a certain television show and then making their judgment based upon those two or three visual encounters. What parents fail to realize is that one episode missed is the one that teaches or instills an un-Godly or non-Christian belief, statement or principle.

I know some of you are saying that it doesn't take all of that, or it is not that serious, but if you are the one saying that then you are the parent I am speaking of. You are the one who has not taken parenthood to the next level. You are the one who needs to tighten up on those loose parenting behaviors to match the unlimited distractions of this day in age. You cannot raise your child like you were raised in the days of old. Our children have so much more they are exposed to in today's world so it is that serious if you really think about it. It is that deep and it does take all of that to make sure we save our children from the clutches of this world. This is why the Christian belief has to be taken wholeheartedly. We are born into sin; therefore we are attracted to sin from birth.

Why do you think it is easier for children to take hold of the negative things faster than the positive? Have you ever been around a child whose parents listen to Gospel music all the time but the one time the child hears a rap song, the child has immediately committed the hook of that song to memory? How about cursing? You can be a well-spoken individual most of the time around your child, but the one time you slip and curse in their presence you find them repeating that same word at the worst time. Then you look astonished to the "accuser" at the thought of your little angel cursing. The accuser asks your child, "Where did you learn that word from?" At that very moment, the parent is reminded of the exact time and day of the mistake THEY made by adding a new word into their little angel's vocabulary.

You must be on your game 24/7 in order to be sure the parent-child relationship is a success. Some of you reading this may also think this is impossible to accomplish, but let me remind you that nothing is impossible to those who believe in the God of the Christian faith (Mark 9:23). Together we will raise a generation that will be pleasing unto God. We just need to do some self-evaluating first! Psalm 127:4 says, "As arrows in the hand of a mighty warrior, so are the children of youth." This verse equates children to arrows in a mighty warrior's hand; but let us be clear that not all adults these days are considered mighty, and neither are they considered to be warriors. It is a sad reality that most adults today cannot be trusted with our beloved community youth let alone their own. The excuse I hear from most is, "Children do not come with an instruction manual." We have a manual called the Holy Bible which teaches us everything about life we need to know in order for parents to be successful.

One verse I hear most from parents is Ephesians 6:1, "Children, obey your parents in the Lord: for this is right," or Colossians 3:20, "Children, obey your parents in all things: for this is well pleasing unto the Lord." I just wish the search for the success of a parent-child relationship went beyond two verses. The Bible goes on to teach in Ephesians 6:4, "And, ye fathers, provoke not your children to wrath: but bring them up in the nurture and admonition of the Lord." Colossians 3.21 also says, "Fathers, provoke not your children to anger, lest they be discouraged," (KJV).

I am currently reading a phenomenal book called *Crazy Love: Overwhelmed by a Relentless God* by Francis Chan. In this book Chan describes the relationship between him and his biological father and how it internally affected his spiritual relationship with his heavenly Father. Chan spoke about how his dad never showed him any affection in public nor did he in private. His dad was only passionate towards him during times of strong discipline and irritation. Chan found himself in an emotional prison and the warden was his own father. Chan walked around the home with only one goal--not to irritate or upset his dad because his dad would drastically punish him. What kind of father is this? Chan stated, "I felt unwanted by my dad, I never carried on a meaningful conversation with my dad and when he died at the age of 12…I felt a sense of relief," (Chan 2010). WOW!

Chan, if you are reading this book my brother, I am so sorry you had to deal with a father like that. Francis Chan made it clear that all of the emotions he developed towards his earthly father transferred to the way he received love from his heavenly Father. Listen dads. You have a very important job in raising your child through effective communication and maximized teaching moments throughout each stage of your child's life. We must be able to trust you with this responsibility so step it up and understand how important your job is! Even though this statement towards fathers is true, it is easier said than done.

The morals of today's adult have changed for the worst. Truth be told, parents today are terrified to allow their child under the age of thirteen further than the driveway of the house due to the amount of crime and unfamiliarity of other adults in the neighborhood. Too many times we think that everyone has our best interest in mind. We believe that nothing is going to happen to our child because everyone knows how crazy we are. Or maybe, you think since you have prayed for protection over your child there is no need for any further concern. If you believe any of these statements to be true, you are sadly mistaken. Yes, God will take care of your child, but through the avenue of common sense.

What has this world come to? Where did we go wrong? The times of trusting the geographical village have been snatched from under our noses and we as parents need to open our eyes to this obvious truth and adjust our mindsets. Some parents still believe that they can trust other parents in their neighborhood—they are wrong. Why? Because the geographical village has holes in it! These holes have become so enormous; humpty dumpty could fit through them. These holes have been successfully created by the devil just to trap our kids into molestation, rape, drugs, alcoholism, gangs, mischief and just plain rebellion from God.

Remember that verse that says, "Train up a child in the way he should go…?" Well the devil believes very strongly in that verse also. The only thing is, he wants to train your child in sinful things early in life so when their age has multiplied, the child will not depart from passionately seeking ungodliness. The enemy wants his village to expose your child to pornography so sexual urges will penetrate their hearts as early as possible. The enemy wants his village to expose your child to a belief system that goes against everything the Bible says and to accomplish this goal when you least expect it. The devil thrives on the element of surprise. His greatest tool is to make you think he does not exist.

An example could be when you walk away from the television and there's a message that insinuates a man and a woman living together without being married is acceptable. What about in that one second you fall asleep and your son is watching a *Will and Grace* commercial that suggests two men being together is normal? The power behind a parent managing what goes into the child's eye-gate and ear-gate is gigantically important. So, when a message is given through the many avenues of communication, we arc there to immediately share with our child that what they saw or what was heard is not Godly. We call this a, "Teaching Moment!" This is what I mean by maximizing every teaching moment to the best of your ability. I know this may seem like a lot for a person to accomplish, but I believe the effort is worth the result of having a spiritually driven, well informed child.

Remember that to kill, to steal and to destroy is the primary strategy of our enemy (John 10:10). The devil travels throughout the earth seeking whom he may devour. So think about it. I know it sounds elementary, but if the enemy wants to be successful in killing the seed of our faith, he will attack us while we are young. If he can get you while you are young then he knows you will deal with struggles the remainder of your adult life. If you don't believe me, ask yourself! Look back into your own life and think about those things you were exposed to as child that you still struggle with today. He wants to plant a seed in your heart, early! For example, the seed of sexuality will expose you to sexual things early in life and will eventually cause major problems in future relationships, if not all of them.

The seed of addiction keeps you dependent on something that can only give you limited pleasure instead of being totally dependent on a God who can bring you unspeakable and unlimited joy. It is all an attack and your child is the prey. The devil has enhanced his level of attack because he knows he does not have much time left. He knew how important the village was to us long ago so the enemy perverted the geographical village. He discredited the geographical village. He downgraded the geographical village and it can no longer be trusted by those who once believed in this very concept. Now, I would like to suggest and defend that the village is still the answer-- just not the village we once knew in the days of old. The village of today must be modified!

The great news is that there is hope and as long as Jesus sits on the throne there will always be hope; but we must first differentiate between who you can and cannot trust within the context of what we call "The Village." In the next chapter I will share with you why our generation has gone so far away from placing their hope in Jesus as our ancestors once did. Without knowing it, we are teaching our youth to question the very Christian principles we have taught them because of the exposure to misplaced hope.

Enjoy…

Chapter Two

Misplaced Hope

(Don't believe the HYPE, believe the HOPE which is in Christ Jesus)

I am currently assigned as the Youth and Young Adult Pastor of Loudoun Bible Church in Ashburn, Virginia under the leadership of Dr. Wayne D. Wyatt. I am also the former Youth Pastor of a prominent church called Sixth Mount Zion Baptist Temple in Hampton, Virginia where the senior Pastor is Reverend Dr. Jerome A. Barber. I have served in Youth Ministry for over 10 years. Surely some of you are wondering what gives this young man the right to speak on this subject without a degree in this field. The wisdom I am sharing comes directly from the Lord and several years of experience leading two very successful Youth ministries. Please understand that I do love working with youth, but I must say that it has been the most challenging ministry endeavor I have ever been a part of in my life.

As humans we love to see immediate gratification in ministry. We want to see the seeds that we have planted and watered grow into beautiful trees that produce much fruit; this is what pleases the Father according to scripture (John 15:8). The challenging part about youth is that you may not ever see the seed you planted grow unless he or she comes back as an adult and shares with you how you have blessed them in their childhood years.

On January 12, 2011 my whole perspective on child development shifted. This is the day my son, Rufus H. Reddick IV. was born. And from that very day I declared that I would never be the same. I thought the love, the passion, the drive, and the energy I put into youth under my leadership and influence in youth ministry was what could be transferred into the development of my own son. Boy was I wrong! Raising my son is so much more intense than I could have ever imagined; there is much more on the line. This is my flesh and blood we are talking about and my primary responsibility is for him not to be fooled by the misleading hopes of this world.

This realization happened when a good friend of mine named Darren Swann called me one day when my wife was pregnant and shared a powerful perspective on parenthood. He said,
"Rufus, the love you have for your wife is a special kind of love that you should always cherish, but the love you will have for your son is

a totally different type of love. See, your wife came to you non-dependent, already thinking for herself, and already established in certain areas of her life. But your son will be totally dependent upon you. Everything you do, everything you say and everything you expose him to will determine what kind of man he will grow up to be. Make sure you do the right thing by him at all times."

This conversation blessed my life tremendously as a soon-to-be Dad. *Darren, if you are reading this book my brother, I want to thank you publicly! You planted a fruitful seed in me that will never die. You inspired this chapter.*

Hope is something that we have allowed to be raped, disgraced and stripped of its purity from its originator. Hope has been an avenue or boulevard that leads to a dead end for those who have decided to place it into the wrong hands. For individuals who have never been exposed to Godly perspective or biblical teaching, I can understand why it is easy for you to place something so important such as hope in the hands of another. But for the believer, it baffles me how easily we place our hope into a limited vessel created by this world or this culture. Let me give you an example. You send your child to Karate class, hoping this experience will create a sense of discipline and structure for your child. Or maybe you encourage him to go to a summer camp, hoping this experience will enhance the child's social skills.

Most parents expose their children to neighborhood schools in hopes that this will improve their ability to learn, to share with other kids, and to develop the kind of mindset that will allow room for immediate or long term success. Other strategies could be sending children to different leadership programs, hoping this will ignite certain skill sets and help them find the abilities that are hidden within. On the other hand, some parents drop their children off in front of the cable network called *Nickelodeon* after coming home from a long day's work, hoping the elected program on television will teach something educational while the mom or dad takes a breather or a nap.

Please do not misunderstand my view point here because I wholeheartedly agree with exposing children to different opportunities that will enrich them in different ways. I totally agree with all of the above ways to better your child. The issue lies in placing hope in these specific opportunities for the sole and complete development of our children.

One day I was watching the *Bernie Mac* television show and Bernie decided to expose his nephew Jordan to his first barber shop experience. Now even though little Jordan was excited about the idea and Bernie Mac was equally excited in exposing Jordan to what his uncle thought every young man should experience, he never took into account what Jordan would take from the experience himself. See, Bernie wanted Jordan to see how men interact with one another.

Bernie wanted Jordan to see how much fun the barbershop can be when men get together—here is a spccial union that develops within. Little did he know, Jordan took on certain characteristics that Bernie never intended for him to have! Jordan was using foul language and making inappropriate jokes—all things he heard from the barber shop. What Bernie wanted Jordan to get out of the whole experience was not exactly what Jordan took from the experience (Willmore 2006).

There has to be a foundation built within the child before the exposure to stronger influence takes place. The powerful content in the words, "Train up a child in the way he should go, and when he is old he will not depart," is this: the training is parallel to the meaning of giving that child a strong foundation before releasing the child to be exposed to anything else in this world. As much as I cannot wait to release my child to all the wonderful opportunities in life that will teach him things I cannot, I want to first make sure his foundation is strong to the best of my ability.

Think about it. You decide to send your child off to summer camp—a summer camp you researched on the internet and the reviews were absolutely astounding. It was ranked 1 out of 25 in the state. They have the best counselors and the very best activities above the rest. You sent your child to hands down the top summer camp on this side of heaven according to the statistics and your research. The excitement around the opportunity is almost uncontainable. You want to fast forward to the end of summer just to see the results from all the money you paid for this experience because you just know it will be worth every penny. On the way to the resort you are anticipating what your child will be like after he returns.

All of these plans and expectations run through your mind. Excitement continues to race through your veins as you pull up to the entrance. You give your sweet, innocent baby a kiss goodbye hoping they will be alright. Three months have passed and it is now time to pick up your baby from summer camp, but you soon find out that your baby is not a baby anymore. The child that jumps in the back of the pick-up truck is not the child you dropped off. You hoped for the best but ended up with something worst. He went to the camp acting one way and comes home acting another. You are in awe because you cannot understand why your baby has changed so drastically and not for the better. This is because the influences in your child's life have shifted into the hands of a person you really did not know for three straight months. You did not know what the counselors believed, what their character was about, nor did you know their sinful desires. Now, this possibly jacked up individual, who has a degree in teaching and facilitating youth activities, has been free to influence their personal opinions and values on a child who has no solid foundation. You hoped your child would obtain certain things from this camp, but in addition to the wonderful things the child has learned, you have noticed the child has picked up some bad habits along the way. Now it seems as if the bad habits that he learned have overshadowed the positive. Prior to camp, the parent was never really confident in the foundation set within the child, so the hope was that the camp experience would teach the child something the parent thought they could not.

Mom or dad let me share something with you. If you are not sure about the foundation set within your child and you are not absolutely confident in your child being able to stand for what is right, then please do not send them into the hands of a complete stranger thinking they can create the foundation you never could. The foundation that you will observe created in your child will not be the one you desired in the first place. You will find yourself attempting to re-program your own child.

I will say this…

This does not happen all the time. Sometimes kids come back better than when they left. This is truly a risky chance you take as the adult. Please understand my plight on this matter. I am not speaking against camps, or schools, or any other positive youth program--I went through them myself when I was a kid. I am merely defending the importance of biblical home training first, then outside exposure next, not the other way around.

The foundation must come from the home. The Bible says in Psalm 71:5, "For thou art my hope, O Lord GOD: thou art my trust from my youth." You as the parent must first teach that our hope is in the Lord and in Him, and Him only, we place all of our trust. This can be taught to a child at a very young age. As a matter of fact I implore you to teach this way of thinking while they are young so it will become second nature to them when they become older. The goal is for our children to know who holds the master key to their future-- teaching them from the home how important it is for God to be their hope by instilling Godly and biblical principles from their youth. Do not allow the world to dictate what your child will or will not believe. Help them to know at a young age that, "God is my foundation and no one will deter me from what I believe."

Now, these next few comments you might not like so please proceed with caution...

In my youth, I could not wait for Christmas because I knew that I was a good boy and Santa Clause was going to give me everything I ever wanted (based upon the song we used to sing for Santa that says, "He's making a list, he's checking it twice, he's gonna find out who's naughty or nice. Santa Clause is coming to town)." I would help my mother decorate the tree with Santa on my mind. I would help her place all the Christmas cards around the house, with Santa in mind. Honestly, all I really was looking forward to was receiving my gifts from Santa Clause. I did not find myself caring about the true meaning of Christmas or anyone else. Don't get me wrong, I was included in the Christmas play at my church and memorized my parts like a good little boy. I knew the story of Jesus' birth and how He was born in a manger because there was no room in the inn. All in all, Santa Clause was the highlight of Christmas for me and nothing else.

The night before Christmas I would place cookies and milk out on the kitchen counter so that my best friend Santa Clause could have something to eat while he left behind everything I requested. My intent was to make sure I made Santa happy to return the favor of making me so happy. Yeah man, I was a good boy so that Santa would have my gift on his list and under our family Christmas tree. The last thing that was on my mind before I went to sleep was Santa and the first thing I could think about waking up on Christmas day was Santa. So when it was present opening time, I found myself thanking Santa even before I thanked anyone else. Shoot, thanking God was the last thing on my mind.

As I got older, I learned through my parents that Santa Clause was not real and it hurt me tremendously. In my mind he became an icon and was the only reason I got excited during Christmas time. When I found out the truth, I was disappointed in my mom for lying to me all those years. As time passed, Christmas became dull to me. Eventually after learning the truth and allowing myself to forgive, only then was I able to learn the real meaning of CHRISTmas. It was all about the birth of Jesus Christ and not about me receiving gifts from an oversized man who can't even fit down the chimney!

With Santa out of the picture, I could now see that Jesus was enough for me to become interested again in this holiday season. The more and more I learned about the true meaning from my parents, the more excited I became about CHRISTmas all over again, but this time for the right reason. Christmas became more meaningful to me. I wish I knew the real reason from the beginning instead of going through the frustrations and the disappointment of Santa Clause not being real.

Let me tell you about another killer. I can remember the times I would lose a tooth, place that tooth under my pillow and in the morning I would have money in the place of the tooth I placed there the night before. This process was very exciting to me, almost to the point where I would find myself attempting to pull teeth out of my mouth that weren't even lose just to get more money waiting for me under my pillow. Shoot, I did not have the joy of believing in Santa Clause anymore so this gave me another fantasy to hold on to.

I thought the world of the tooth fairy. All I had to do was put a tooth under the pillow and I would get a dollar. How easy was that? Santa wasn't real but at least I still had the tooth fairy. Little did I know that my beloved mother was the tooth fairy! I was not really upset finding out that it was my mother instead of a magical tooth fairy as long as I still received the money under the pillow. The messed up part about the whole thing was that when she told me the truth, she stopped placing money under my pillow. I was devastated and disappointed all over again!

I began to question everything after I found out about Santa and the tooth fairy. It caused me to even question my faith about God for a while. It led me to think that if these two iconic figures in my life were no longer real and was just a fairy tale for a short while…could God be the same way?

What if I told you that allowing your child to place their hope in hopeless situations will delay their destiny and purpose in Christ Jesus? What if the truth was told from the very beginning? How closer to my calling would I have been? One thing I know is this: children love to daydream and play "make believe." There is something inside of a child and even some parents that influence the need to step away from reality and into a world of fantasy. Why do you think addictions are so prevalent? Drugs have the ability to take you away from current problems or situations and into a place of temporary enjoyment. Addictions continue because the person wants to feel the way they felt during the first experience all the time.

What if parents taught from the very beginning of childhood to place hope in Jesus Christ, rather than conditioning them to place hope in temporary things like make believe characters? If that were the case, it would not be so easy for a person to rely on worldly addictions but on the contrary addict themselves to the Lord because He was the foundation set from their youth. I am sure all of this is easier said than done, but it is worth a try, don't you think?

The Bible has awesome stories little kids can use in their fantasy world, so why not use them? I know, I know, I know. I am sure you are thinking it is not that serious. You may probably say that I am taking innocent childhood fun away--that allowing children to imagine Santa or the tooth fairy is not going to hurt anything or anyone. If this is you, you are sadly mistaken.

One more—the Easter Bunny! Some believers still call the day we celebrate Jesus Christ's rising, "Easter Sunday." It should be called "Resurrection Sunday!" Do we not see the intelligent strategy of the enemy and how he has infiltrated our hearts away from God? Now is the time to STOP believing in the HYPE of this world and begin believing and instilling in our youth the HOPE of Jesus Christ. Start teaching our children the real meaning of Christmas without including the word SANTA which unscrambled spells out another word, SATAN!

Help our youth fully appreciate the birth of our Savior. Understand that CHRISTmas is about giving and not receiving! Share with our children that the tooth fairy is not your "Jehovah Jireh" my provider, God is (Genesis 22:14)! Easter Sunday does not exist to have Easter egg hunts and for a bunny to jump around and give children candy. It is unequivocally about a man named Jesus who came to save us from the clutches of sin. He was a man who died so that we might have the gift of eternal life and to celebrate a man who rose with ALL power in His hand. Nothing more, nothing less.

We should no longer misguide our hope, but place our hope in the hands of the one who cannot and will not fail. Placing our hope where hope belongs—in God! The Bible says to trust in the Lord with ALL thine heart (Proverbs 3:5). Most people overlook the key word in that scripture-- ALL! All does not mean some times or most times—it means 100 percent of the time. When we begin to teach our kids this from their youth they will not be so easily tossed and driven by the frustrations or distractions of this world. When we begin to show them that God is the only one who can heal and deliver, our children will be able to stand boldly in the face of adversities and from their hearts say Psalm 23:1, “The Lord is my Shepherd I shall not want.” So my beloved, don’t believe the hype, believe in the only hope that will last which is in Christ Jesus!

Now that I have your undivided attention, we can start the process of creating your personal village. Hold on to your hats!

Chapter Three

The Power of a Seed

The first two chapters were and will be very important to this whole process in creating your own village. With anything, you must build a strong foundation before the growing process can take place. Now don't get me wrong, you can attempt these principles without rearranging your parenting game plan. Just understand this: your mindset and where you stand on spiritual matters has to be in line with God's word or this will not work for you long term. The enemy wants you to believe that you can do this all on your own but that is nowhere near the case. It might work for a short while from just the appearance but trust me, without the Lord--it will be much harder than it should. So your greatest chance in creating your village successfully and for eternity is to do this God's way. By placing all of your trust in the Lord (Chapter One) and teaching your children to place their hope in the Lord (Chapter Two). Set this foundation and you cannot lose!

Okay, here we go…

As I mentioned in the first chapter, the geographical village cannot be trusted due to the moral holes that society has allowed to grow larger and larger in our communities. Thank God there is a solution. The village is still the answer, but just not the geographical village such as your neighborhoods and/or community. You must be proactive in knowing what type of environments you want your child to be exposed to and who you want speaking into your child's life.

One thing I really want you to see in this chapter is how important and how powerful a seed is. A seed is most important to any type of growth in the physical and in the spiritual. In order for a seed to grow it must be planted and watered in order for increase to come from that seed. How amazing it is for a small seed to create an enormous tree such as the ones we see on the side of the roads as we drive on our daily route to work or to school. Nature never ceases to amaze me and neither does the potential of just one seed.

The Bible says, "One plants, one waters and God gives the increase," (1 Corinthians 3:7-8). My only concern is what seeds are being planted in your child and by whom? This is a question one should ask every single day and with every single person that comes in contact with your child. See, here is the deal. There are so many kinds of seeds that try to find their way onto the soil of your children's soul. The seed of negativity, the seed of low self-esteem, the seed of neglect, the seed of insecurity, the seed of lust, the seed of depression, the seed of suicide, the seed of homosexuality, etc. I can go on and on, but I think you get the picture.

I always tell this to the parents in our Youth Ministry, "God sends people into your lives to help build your child, but also keep in mind that the devil dispatches his own group of people in order to kill, steal and destroy that same child." The goal for the enemy is to never allow your child to figure out their true identity in Christ Jesus. So in order for the enemy to complete this task, people will begin to rise up in the lives of the parent in order to gain the type of influence over the child they were assigned by the enemy to destroy.

One thing I have learned about a terrorist from being in the military is that in order to carry out the perfect attack, one must be very patient and strategic in their approach. Take a look at the shooting that transpired on Fort Hood Military Base in Texas on November 5, 2009. An army officer by the name of Nidal Malik Hasan (who earned the rank of Major and served as the base psychiatrist) fatally shot 13 people and injured more than thirty others. This event was recorded as the worst shooting to ever take place on a military base. Six years before the shooting, concerns arose about certain comments Hasan made concerning America's fight in Iraq and Afghanistan, but nothing was taken too seriously. In that six year period, the seeds of hate toward America were watered each day. The very seed that was planted in his spirit as a young boy after his country became victim to American attack contributed to his mindset. He took the time to educate himself and put himself into a place of influence so his plan could work to perfection (Nidal Hasan).

This is a wonderful example of how patient the enemy is and how early he will plant seeds in people so they can perfectly situate themselves to carry out his demonic plan. The enemy will stop at nothing to take the innocence and the potential from your child's life. He knows if he can plant seeds of hate and destruction in the early years, the easier it will be to convince the child to help orchestrate a plan of destruction to themselves or to someone else. It all begins with one seed. Truthfully, you cannot stop every negative seed from entering your child's spirit. The strategy we take toward the negative is to overly expose them with positive ones and using the negative responses as a teaching moment of how they should not respond to life. It is very important to share with them your past mistakes so they will not always feel as if they have become the worst person in the world when they make a mistake.

Young people are always under the impression that they are the only ones who have experienced something, especially when it comes to the negative, but by helping them to understand that mistakes are made by all of us allows them to feel accompanied in their tragedies. The worst thing you can feel when you have made a mistake is "alone." The seed you want to plant in your child is to ensure they do not feel all by themselves and if they need to talk about anything, you are there to listen without judgment. A good friend of mine who is a single parent shared with me a wonderful concept that she uses with her children. The concept she mentioned to me is called the "judge free zone." It is a time of the day, typically at night, where each child has the opportunity to share something that Mom cannot be upset about or punish them about. It is a time where that child can be completely honest and there is nothing that can happen to them. Now, let's be honest here— at times she became very angry inside, but she promised that nothing will be held against them. This concept caused great communication between the children and the parent. This may not work for you but the point of me bringing it up is to reveal the power of positive communication. Even though you may not be the person your child reveals secrets to, you better believe there is someone they have chosen to share these secrets. Who your child communicates their heart to is the very person who will have the influence to create a monster or an angel.

Short story...

Charlie and Leslie have been trying to have a baby now for about 3 years. Charlie is looking for a son while Leslie really does not mind either way. She is just excited about having a child, especially since this might be her last chance to have a baby at her age. Leslie just turned 39 and she is concerned about her body being able to carry the baby to full term without any complications.

Unlike Charlie, Leslie has a strong support system because Leslie loves to meet new people. Charlie is pretty social too but not as social as his wife Leslie. Leslie has a gift for helping people and at times she confuses her role in people's lives because of how relational she is with others. If someone has a problem and brings that problem to Leslie, she will try everything in her power to find a solution for their situation. Charlie always tells Leslie to keep her guard up when it comes to people, but Leslie has always been the kind of woman who had to learn on her own.

Fast forward and four months have passed, and the beautiful couple has just been informed that they will be having a baby! Charlie is blown away that his first born will be a boy while Leslie is very emotional due to the nervousness of becoming a mother. During the pregnancy Leslie has befriended a group of ladies who Charlie does not approve of based upon his personal encounter with the ladies. Charlie begins to see certain personality traits in Leslie's new friends and is beginning to worry that these ladies will have a negative impact on his wife.

Charlie mentioned his feelings to Leslie, but of course Leslie blew him off and did not listen. She felt that Charlie was just being his normal judgmental self. Charlie knew that this was a sensitive subject for his wife so he never brought her friends up again. The baby is now 15 years old and Leslie's friends are still around, while Charlie still does not approve after multiple attempts to accept them. Leslie created a village for their son and Charlie allowed an unapproved village to be created around his son. The personality issues that Charlie noticed in Leslie's friends from the very beginning are the same kind of personality issues he and his wife are fighting against with their son now.

This is actually a true story that I have seen a many times in my Youth Ministry. It is sad to see parents become more concerned about their own social relationships rather than placing their child around people who have the things they desire their children to develop. Remember, you should always want your child to have or be exposed to more than what you were exposed to in order to provide that child with multiple options in life versus the limited options you might have been given. So if your friends are ghetto, confrontational, homosexual, broke, uneducated, non-believers or addicts, you better believe your child will inherit those characteristics. Why you might say? Well, since those are your friends, those are your child's make-believe aunts and uncles. They are the ones who have developed trust in your child based upon them being around the house the majority of the time. This is the person that your child will share their secrets with concerning their life.

So let me ask you this. Do you trust the advice of the friends you have placed around your child? Do you think that if a question arose from your child to that adult, would the adult tell your child what you would like them to know? If not, re-create your village. If you don't like the word re-create than use this one—*modify* your village!

Chapter Four

Creating/Modifying a Village

The village concept is a strategy that has been lost in the 21st Century mindset of the parent. The misconception of parenting is thinking that we can accomplish raising a child without the help of others. Our community has tried to convince us to believe that you can raise a productive child with the help of just anybody in your circle. If you believe either of those two you are setting yourself up for the worst case scenario.

The strategy to create a village that your child will not just survive in, but rather thrive in, is equivalent to the hiring strategy that an intelligent business owner may make to help build a brand new company. I heard a very successful Pastor say, "When the church went from two-hundred people to seven-thousand people in one year, I decided that I needed help, but I did not hire based on the need. I hired base upon my heart and my weaknesses."

This strategy can be just as impactful and helpful to building a community of people around your child to become productive in his or her life. You want people around your child who has your heart. If you are a Christian believer of Jesus Christ, you want Christians around your child. This is the thing: you have to trust that whoever gives advice to your child inside your village knows your heart so that your heart will be communicated to that child-- just from another human being. Similar to a business, everyone must know the vision and mission of the organization. As it is for your child, everyone must be brought into the vision and the mission for your child.

In order for the village to have your heart, you must have invested countless hours of time with each person you have chosen. What I don't want you to think is that you must go out and find all new people that you do not even know to be a part of your village. No, that is not what I am saying. I am merely saying that the impactful people that God has already blessed you with during your developmental processes are the same ones that you should expose your child too. A good friend of mine calls this concept, "being a good steward over your relationships." I am speaking of the people that you trust who are like minded and have your best interest at heart.

Try to stay away from those who fall in love with your child and hardly know you. They will begin to share things to your child that might not be according to your expectations for your child. You always want people around who love you first and love your children because of you.

People who love you will always keep your heart at the center of the relationship concerning your child.

I remember a time even before I had children that my oldest nephew Timothy Reddick, Jr. came to visit me while I was the Youth Pastor in Hampton, Virginia. He was there for our Youth New Year's celebration and there was a young lady who was not fond of me at the time. As a matter of fact, we did not get along at all. Her being a part of the Youth Ministry team was the greatest challenge. At the time, she did not like me and honestly, I did not speak of her too kindly either.

Well, when our New Year's celebration came to an end, everyone began to disburse from the building toward their vehicles. I was walking out a little late because I wanted to greet all of the youth and wish them a happy new year, but when I finally came out I saw this woman, who did not like me, standing with my nephew by my vehicle laughing and giggling. Immediately I became very concerned. I could not get to them fast enough so I pushed the emergency siren button on my truck and the alarm went off! They both jumped and looked up at me with a look of confusion. When the young lady saw the look on my face she walked away cautiously because she knew her intentions were not pure. The blessing behind this story is that we have reconciled and are good friends still to this day.

I am sharing this story with you because there will be people who will try and force themselves into becoming an influence in your child's lives who openly do not have good feelings towards you. These people are worse than anyone else because if they accomplish the goal of gaining the trust of your child, they will purposely go against everything you have taught just to get under your skin with no positive regard for the child.

The villagers must have your heart! It took the disciples three years before Jesus felt comfortable leaving them to do the work on their own. Use this concept of time as your gage because it takes time for someone outside of your home to develop the integrity of your heart.

This is why you should begin choosing from people who have already proven themselves to love you. Now everyone that loves you will not love your children, but pay close attention to the ones who automatically present a genuine concern for your child's well-being.

Here is the tricky part, your village may or may not consist of your immediate family. If your parents, brothers or sisters have issues or challenges, then maybe they will not become a part of your village and that is okay. Now understand, your village are people that you trust to watch your child overnight and to speak life into your child outside of your presence. If there are some things going on in mom or dads house that you do not agree with than you will have to do monitored visits with them until things change for the better. Never neglect your child from being a part of their grandparents' lives, but if you don't agree with the lifestyle, I would highly suggest you monitor very closely every visit and debrief the child by using the negative exposure as a teaching moment. This goes the same for the siblings or any other family member you love very much.

This is not personal but rather purposeful. You can't afford for anyone to gain negative influence concerning your child if you can help it. Some people you will not have any control over when it comes to the influence of your child but if you can help it, control it.

Finding a good Youth Ministry…

Finding a church that speaks directly to your child is very important as well. The church must be a place where the Youth Ministry has someone designated specifically for the youth. Most churches have not understood the important fact of investing into the lives of our youth at their church. Most times, you will find churches experimenting with preachers through Youth Ministry. I highly suggest that you sit in on the sermon presentations rendered to your child to ensure it is sound biblical doctrine. The sign of a thriving Youth Ministry is one that is youth- led. What I mean by this statement is this: Youth Ministries where youth are leading and participating in the planning and execution of the ministry. Most youth ministries that are not youth-led are missing the mark dearly because the church has not accepted that they know nothing about youth today. I always tell the kids I minister to, "I may be cool and I may be accepted by you but if you don't tell me how to reach you I won't be impactful."

The only way to effectively reach youth today is for the youth you are leading to tell you how to reach them. If the youth are silent and acting as if they are robots just doing what they have been told by the adults and not allowed to express their creativity, then the ministry is shallow and it has no depth. What youth generally learn in this type of environment is how to play church versus becoming the Church Christ is coming to take home to glory.

The goal of a youth-led ministry is to empower the youth to value the gifts God has given them and how God made them—fearfully and wonderfully! Also, to connect that gift to Christ as early as possible because truth be told, some of the youth will not understand Christ to be their Savior until they become older, but at the least they will know to offer that gift to Christ if nothing else. The ultimate prayer is that youth learn to develop an intimate relationship with Christ through their gifts.

What you must not forget when it comes to creating your village is this: you are the most important villager in that village. Creating a village does not exclude you from the village. On the contrary, you are the one that gives life or takes life away from the village. The parent/guardian is the deciding factor of what the village does and how far the village goes. Without the heart, the body does not live. So without you, the village does not survive effectively. If the heart of the village is not present, multiple heads are created and anything with more than one head is a monster.

You don't want to become what I call the "drop the ball" parent. This is the kind of parent who drops the ball (child) off to different activities within their village and expects everyone else to teach their child what they should be teaching the child themselves. Being an intricate part of your child's activities will speak volumes not only to your child, but to the ones who are trying to negatively influence the child. Pastor Reverend Doctor Jerome A. Barber told me something that I will never forget concerning people you are counting on to produce something great. He said, "What you don't inspect, people will not respect. This screams true to the village you create. You must take the time to inspect what the village is saying and what the village is doing. Most importantly, you must also inspect how the village is living.

This brings me to my final point. Some people will not remain in your village because life happens and perspectives change. Just because your favorite villager for 10 years has been your most trusted advisor and mentor for your child, does not mean that the villager's life can't take a turn for the worst and his or her perspective about life could change.

Please don't get me wrong. We should not just throw people away just because they have hit a hard time in their lives. In moments such as these we should rally together even the more but that does not mean that person stays a part of your village. This is a transition that may be hard for everyone, but it has to be a decision that is made for the betterment of the child. That is a great opportunity for the child to support the villager, while the parent shares the turn in their life and why it is important to pray for them until they regain their stability. Okay, let me give you an example…

Short story…

John and Ashley have been married for ten years. These two beautiful people have one child who has his father's name--John. John, Jr. is his dad's pride and joy. John, Sr. has totally bought into the village concepts and has created a productive village with the help of his beautiful wife. One of the villagers is his Uncle Louis. Uncle Louis was a father figure to John, Sr., so he could not think of any other man to help raise his only son. Uncle Louis was so excited about the opportunity to become a role model for not only John, Sr. but also John, Jr. Over the course of four years Uncle Louis started going down a path of bad decisions and could not seem to get himself together. John, Sr. reached out to him multiple times but Uncle Louis would not respond. During the tenure of Uncle Louis being a role model for John, Jr. they created a relational moment between the two of them. John, Jr. would always go and spend the third weekend with Uncle Louis, but after numerous times of attempting to contact Uncle Louis, John, Sr. decided that he would stop by and check on him.

Well, when John, Sr. and John, Jr. arrived they found Uncle Louis on his couch drunk and high on cocaine. At that moment both were very concerned and immediately began assisting Uncle Louis through his recovery process. During the process, Uncle Louis just did not seem to want to change after numerous attempts from John, Sr. seeking to help him. John, Sr. had to make the hardest decision of his life. He had to remove Uncle Louis from his son's life as his primary villager, but rather he made his son a distant villager for his Uncle Louis. They began to pray for Uncle Louis from a distance until Uncle Louis was ready to make that change.

This is a true story!

Even though you may think you have created the greatest village for your child, the work is never over. After creating the village you must also monitor the village to ensure the villagers are maintaining the type of progress and stability you want your child exposed too. As I said in the previous chapters, some Christians may even say that all you have to do is trust God and pray for your children but I beg to differ. I believe that God will protect our children if we trust Him, but I also believe that He has granted us the authority to do the best that we can with what He has blessed us with. If we are faithful over the things that only we can do than God will in turn release the great things that only He can release into our lives. Modify your village before it is too late!

Chapter Five

Feeding the Village

It would be a shame to think that this model will only benefit the one creating the village as well as the child inside this modified village. I would rather help you understand an additional truth. Now don't get me wrong, creating the village is primary, but feeding the village is critical. There should always be time spent with your villagers to ensure they are still maintaining your expectations concerning the mindset required for your child and to also ensure they are getting the support they need to become better themselves. What you pour into your village is what will be poured into your child. The challenge with this specific responsibility is that time is not something a lot of us have. So time spent with your village should never be time wasted. Here are some specific things you want to focus on when you are spending time with your villagers... Empower them! The village should always understand the importance of their presence being in your child's life as well as yours.

One of my favorite movies that reveals the greatest mentor-to-mentee village relationship is Karate Kid. Mr. Miyagi was the **MAN** and he loved him some Daniel son! He would look after Daniel as if he was his own son. He taught young Daniel how to be a man, a champion and a good person. Mr. Miyagi taught Daniel discipline and how to reach down into himself and become something greater than what people saw on the outside. Daniel did not have a muscular outer appearance, college education, nor did he have eloquence of speech, but yet and still Mr. Miyagi understood that Daniel could be something great. Daniel's mother was the mastermind behind the whole operation. She knew her limits and saw Mr. Miyagi's strengths and influence over her son. This allowed Daniel to become someone his mother could not develop on her own and that was a man with confidence (The Karate Kid).

A boy must see a man doing man things in order for him to become who he was originally designed to become. This does not mean a woman cannot raise a man because I have seen some women raise awesome men, but these specific women were very strategic in placing great men in front of her sons because there were just some things he needed to hear from someone who looked like he did.

Educate them! The village must be educated on the current mindset and atmosphere you seek to develop around your child. Help them to understand what the current issues are concerning your child. If your child is dealing with behavioral, learning, listening or social challenges this is the time to really educate your village so that everyone can have the same goal and focus concerning your child. As you know, most children listen to advice outside the home quicker than they do inside the home. This is why your village must be in agreement with your current position and the goal is to ensure the child is impacted from every side. I call this "Gang Support." This is where the village has become so focused and fixed on the goal that the effort from each component can be looked upon as very aggressive behavior. The aggressiveness is what is needed to match or exceed the approach the devil and/or the world has for our children. If we don't start fighting just as hard as our adversary we are positioning our children for failure.

Equip them! You must pray for your villagers. Every name in their house should be called out daily in prayer from your lips. You want the Spirit of God to rest, rule and abide in the house and heart of your villagers. Prayer will equip those you have chosen to maintain the stability and consistency needed for your child to develop properly. Not only will it be a blessing for your child but it should benefit the house of the villager. Prayer will also keep you in tune with what the villager is in need of at the moment to maintain good, positive, Christian living. Whoever has the greatest influence in the house of your villager is the one you should be in contact with on a regular basis. Not to ask anything from them, but to see if there is anything you can do for them. It is vital to equip your village with the kind of love that you want shown to your children. You should equip your village with the kind of concern and care you want shown to your children. By doing this, you are arming your village with the very tools that will help them become better people for themselves and most importantly, your child. The Bible says to give and it shall be given back to you pressed down, shaken together and running over shall others give to you (Luke 6:38).

When you understand the concept of giving and impart that concept into your village you will immediately begin seeing a return on your investment. People don't necessarily remember what you have said, people will not always remember what you have done for them, but rather, people will remember very clearly how you made them feel (Maya Angelou Quotes). You can have a beautiful crystal glass in front of you, but if there is nothing inside that glass you will never be able to enjoy the purpose behind why that glass was created. However, when you pour into the glass what you want to receive out of it then you will start enjoying that in which you have poured inside. Your village should be able to count on you just as much as you have counted on them. Any relationship where there is no reciprocity will eventually fade and die, but when both parties are feeling loved and appreciated the atmosphere becomes that much more affective towards the development of your child.

God has truly gifted me with a heart for the spiritual development of our children. My prayer is that you do everything in your power to change the way we have been doing things concerning our children. The village is still the answer—just modify it to impact our children.

Works Cited

Chan, Francis, and Danae Yankoski. *Crazy Love: Overwhelmed by a Relentless God*. N.p.: n.p., 2010. Print.

The Holy Bible: New American Standard. New York: American Bible Society, 2000. Print.

The Karate Kid. Swank, 1985. DVD.

"Maya Angelou Quotes." *GoodReads*. Good Reads, Inc., 2015. Web.

"Nidal Hasan Sentenced to Death for Fort Hood Shooting Rampage." *Washington Post*. The Washington Post, 28 Aug. 2015. Web. 15 Aug. 2015.

Willmore, Larry. *Bernie Mac Show*. Wilmore Films. 2006. Television.

About the Author

Rufus H. Reddick, III.

Rufus H. Reddick, III. is the current Youth and Young Adult Pastor of Loudoun Bible Church in Ashburn, Virginia under the leadership of Reverend Dr. Wayne D. Wyatt and the immediate past Youth Pastor of Sixth Mount Zion Baptist Temple, a strong growing congregation in Hampton, Virginia under the leadership of Rev. Dr. Jerome A. Barber. He is the fifth-born child to Pastor John Snell and Dorothy R. Snell. The Cleveland, Ohio native is currently serving his country and has so far dedicated seventeen years to the United States Navy. His life motto is, "When you live on PURPOSE you will never lose the required passion to encourage God's people."

While working for the Unites States Navy, Minister Reddick, III. won the distinction of being selected Sailor of the Year for his tremendous work ethic, integrity and dedication in 2004, 2010 and 2013. Through God's grace, he has also achieved the rank of a Chief Petty Officer and uses this position to further God's kingdom agenda inside of the military. While working in a demanding Naval career, he continues his journey and passion for youth and young adult ministry.

Minister Reddick is married to the former Tiara A. Anderson. Together they are the proud parents of two wonderful children: Rufus H. Reddick, IV. and Reagan Brielle Reddick.

www.purethoughtspublishingllc.com

Made in the USA
Middletown, DE
17 October 2015